# Our *Way* Home

# Our *Way* Home

Reimagining an American Farmhouse

**Heide Hendricks and Rafe Churchill**
With Laura Chávez Silverman
Photography by Chris Mottalini

**RIZZOLI**
NEW YORK

New York · Paris · London · Milan

# Contents

# *Foreword*

The word I've often used to describe my favorite quality in the work of Hendricks Churchill is *humanity*—largely because of Heide and Rafe's knack for creating interiors that feel layered, lived in, and loved from the moment the key turns in a client's door.

But perhaps another apt word would be *alchemy*, reliant as Hendricks Churchill's interiors are on transformation and unlikely combinations. In a Hendricks Churchill home, an antique bench may find new life in a reading room, its wood restored and given new luster; a vintage Moroccan dhurrie may set the stage for a custom sofa upholstered in a sumptuous wool. Eras, colors, prints, and material palettes spark against each other in surprising, intelligent ways that can seem more like sorcery than like the decorating handiwork of mere mortals. The pages that follow capture that magic and showcase the unpretentiousness and love of craft that caught my attention when I became acquainted with the studio's work years ago.

For my first official issue as editor in chief at *Elle Decor*—the magazine's March 2021 edition—I hoped to present a case for interior design and decoration as an important reflection of the culture at large, outside the bubble of the industry, and make the argument for comfort and style at home as the ultimate luxury (especially in those anxious early days of the Covid-19 pandemic). To help me make the case, we included a Greek Revival house in Farmington, Connecticut, smartly revamped by Hendricks Churchill, for a couple in the art world and their two young children. Like all of the homes in the issue, I felt it embodied my ethos for this new chapter in the magazine's history. But beyond the ideas that underpin Hendricks Churchill's work and the ways those ideas dovetailed with my own fascinations and interests, I will admit: the house in Farmington simply made me want to move in. You'll likely want to do the same after joining Heide and Rafe on this journey about their own home, Ellsworth.

Asad Syrkett
Editor in Chief, *Elle Decor*

# Introduction

This book is an invitation: a door thrown open to a house, to a way of life, and to the people who built them. It is the story of Ellsworth, an 1871 farmhouse in the northwest corner of Litchfield County, Connecticut, and of Heide Hendricks and Rafe Churchill, the partners in work and life who restored it to its current glory. They named the house after the hilltop hamlet in which it sits, referred to by G. F. Goodenough in the 1900 edition of his book on Ellsworth, Connecticut, as a place where "nature set it off by itself, for to reach it from anywhere but the sky, you must rise." Originally established as a working dairy farm with multiple barns, the property was still inhabited by the elderly gentleman who had lived there for fifty years when Rafe first set eyes on the house in 2003. Its regal presence, bucolic setting, and sense of history spoke to him on a visceral level. Despite the signs of disrepair beginning to show, Rafe and Heide admired the place whenever they passed by (driving around the back roads was how they sometimes got their baby daughter to fall asleep), dreaming of the possibilities but never imagining it might one day be theirs. Having just designed and built a new house of their own in nearby Sharon, it says something that the farmhouse continued to linger in their minds.

From the time they first encountered Ellsworth until the day in 2018 when the stars aligned for them to buy it, Heide, an interior designer, and Rafe, a designer-builder, undertook three major home renovations and moves, had a second child, and worked on a wide range of award-winning design and architectural projects, both locally and in New York City. Over the years, they honed their distinctive aesthetic, developed a collaborative process, and eventually formed a business partnership, Hendricks Churchill, known for a holistic approach to authentic New England houses rich in character and soul. They were also instrumental in reinvigorating Sharon's scenic town green and West Main Street, rehabbing a series of historic yet dilapidated buildings that now houses their office, a barbershop, wine bar, café, and several apartments. All of this meant Rafe and Heide were supremely ready to create their dream home. Having long scrutinized Ellsworth's graceful bones, they were excited to return it to its original state, peeling away work that had been done in the 1960s and '70s to reveal the fine craftsmanship beneath. The two were so aligned in their vision that the entire project took just months.

The house is quintessentially American—honest, gracious, utilitarian—as is the story of Heide and Rafe, two talented individuals who achieved success by virtue of hard work and shared passion. They both grew up in Woodbury, Connecticut, but did not meet until after college. Rafe, descended from three generations of carpenters and builders, was artistically inclined. He studied sculpture and architecture at Bennington College, then dropped out of Cranbrook Academy of Art and turned away from a burgeoning career as an artist toward the more familiar and practical path of a contractor. Heide and her four siblings were raised by bohemian parents in a house they built out of lumber milled from trees on the property and filled with art and eclectic finds from estate sales, flea markets, and thrift shops. After studying art history at Syracuse, she worked for years as a publicist for arts and cultural organizations, expressing her own artistic side through the environments she designed at home. Heide and Rafe, both creative spirits, recognized in each other a shared appreciation for Yankee ingenuity, for the value of artisan craft, and for freedom from convention.

The couple's early years were spent living in Williamsburg, Brooklyn, and renovating a series of small Connecticut properties they managed to buy. Every Friday, they would cash the paychecks from their day jobs and run to the lumberyard for supplies, then they'd spend the entire weekend wielding their power tools. For Heide, it was the first little cottage they transformed into a beautiful home that opened a vision of the future for her, one in which they had agency over their life together. Rafe's passion for making things with his hands, for the simplicity of Shaker design, and for the authenticity of vernacular buildings, was a guiding force in their personal projects (five flipped houses) and in what would ultimately become a joint professional practice.

Ellsworth represents their most seamless and successful collaboration to date. It cemented Heide's career as an interior designer and Rafe's role as both designer and builder. Today, the Hendricks Churchill family—including daughter Hollis, son Rufus, wheaten terrier Daisy, and the family cat, Mr. Biggie—calls Ellsworth home. They have made it possible for the farm to live on. A local farmer cuts and bales the hayfields. There is room for both work and play in the restored barn. Surrounding woodlands are managed with an eye toward improved wildlife habitat. The property is alive with activity.

This is a very personal book, delving into not only the way Heide and Rafe approach design but also how they live in their own home. It represents the synthesis of everything they have learned and the culmination of a journey. The house has become an endless source of inspiration for all their projects, allowing them to work through ideas and test approaches to use of color, scale of furniture, and even unorthodox building techniques. Ellsworth was arguably the first house they viewed as a "forever home," a place where their children might find respite with children of their own. In these pages, you will see Ellsworth through Heide's and Rafe's eyes, progressing through the rooms of their rambling farmhouse and into the grounds beyond. They extend a warm welcome into the spaces where they gather with family and friends, retreat into private moments, wander through the natural setting, and work behind the scenes. Around every corner is a reminder of what home means to Hendricks Churchill: comfort, beauty, color, utility, space, and harmony.

# *Finding* Ellsworth

The hamlet of Ellsworth is located in the northwest corner of Litchfield County, Connecticut, due east of the colonial town of Sharon. A country road winds through old-growth woodlands that give way to acres of open pasture punctuated by long, meandering lines of dry-stone walls. A classic farmhouse, built in 1871 as part of a large dairy farm that closed nearly a century later, sits on thirty-three acres along this quiet road. In front, majestic horse chestnut and maple trees flank the house. Mature fruit trees and grape arbors are visible in back, with open meadows, woods, and wetland beyond.

During the fifteen years that Rafe and Heide admired this stately house and its fairytale setting, it came on the market several times, always for more than they could afford. Apparently, it was beyond what anyone wanted to pay, as it remained unsold. In 2018, the bank finally foreclosed on the property and relisted it for less than half of the previous price. Heide and Rafe immediately made an offer and were thrilled to become the new stewards of a beloved house that had once seemed entirely out of reach. Theirs would be only the fourth family to inhabit Ellsworth since it was built by Joshua Bignall Chaffee.

Though the structure was originally conceived as a humble working farmhouse, it has graceful proportions and finely wrought details that give it presence. The simple floor plan features high-ceilinged rooms that flow from one to the next, illuminated by windows that stream light in from multiple exposures and look out onto sweeping views of the picturesque landscape. The day Heide and Rafe closed on Ellsworth, they walked through each room and made a list of everything they wanted to change. This ranged from removing extra doors to gutting the kitchen to creating a double-height sunroom out of a small barn attached to the main house. Incredibly, by the end of the renovation that initial vision had survived intact.

Like any old house that has been only partially updated over the years, the 2,900-square-foot structure needed lots of work to bring it up to modern living standards. The plumbing, heating, and electrical systems all had to be replaced (and the three chimneys used to vent the seven woodstoves removed), along with roughly half the windows. The house had been reconfigured by the previous owners—including renovated bathrooms, an updated kitchen, and wall-to-wall carpeting from the 1970s—but the underlying craftsmanship had endured. Rafe and Heide decided to expose and refinish the original pine floors and keep whatever early woodwork they could, including the scrollwork on the front porch, and replicate missing pieces of trim wherever necessary. They even tried to retain as much of the original plaster as possible. Crown moldings were installed for consistency with the existing window trim and tall baseboards, adding elegant punctuation to the front rooms and tapering off to a more utilitarian style in the back of the house. When new doors or windows were added, the existing proportions and details were carefully reproduced, except for the entry to the living room, which was widened for a more welcoming feel. The firmly constructed doors have doorknobs smoothed by countless turns of the hand. The staircase banister of perfect geometrical straights and curves ends in the full stop of its sentry newel post.

For the new kitchen, Heide and Rafe designed a room with beadboard paneling, a deep marble sink, and an island topped by a counter of thick white oak. It segues into the dining room, an oversize space that accommodates a long Shaker-style dining table made of tiger maple, as well as a cozy sitting area with a down-filled sofa and vintage armchairs freshly upholstered in custom textiles. The kitchen also opens to an expansive pantry with a door to the back terrace, an adjacent laundry room, and a new mudroom with a cement-tiled floor. Through the mudroom is an area at the back of the house that was once an attached barn with two tiny bedrooms upstairs. (The original chestnut floors were salvaged from there and remilled; these handsome wide planks were repurposed in the front entrance hall.) From this space, Heide and Rafe created a light-drenched, double-height sunroom with exposed beams, radiant heat in the floor, and the only contemporary sliding doors in the house, a concession to maximizing the views and because the narrow room would not accommodate swinging doors.

Off the kitchen is the kind of steep, narrow staircase often found in houses from this era and usually removed in favor of adding more storage space or an extra bathroom. Heide and Rafe have a fondness for just this type of historical detail, so it remains a secondary means of reaching the second floor of Ellsworth,

where all five bedrooms are situated. The stair railing, made of black plumbing pipe, is an insider's reference to the inexpensive option they used in their earlier remodels. It has a utilitarian charm and over time will acquire a burnished patina. At the top of the house was a raw attic, which they decided to finish about halfway through the project. It already had a wide staircase leading up to it and required only minimal framing and drywall. The original windows were a horizontal pocketed style with five panes of glass; Rafe eventually agreed to replace them with larger double-hung windows that Heide felt would be a safer option, as this big room often serves as a refuge and sleepover space for their kids.

Behind the house sits the giant three-bay barn, originally red and now painted a particularly rich and resonant shade of plum that complements the violet undertones in the pale gray covering the house. When Rafe first saw the barn, it was overgrown with vines and had two additions on the side that were collapsing. The top floor was not safe. He replaced the roof, reframed the gable walls and the floor system, and added two layers of sub-floor. Now the upstairs is the ultimate hangout space, complete with vintage sofas, movie projector, and skateboard ramp. Downstairs, the center bay is a garage and the third bay houses Rafe's woodshop and studio.

To these carefully considered and meticulously executed structures, Heide layered on her signature mix of warm, eclectic furnishings—antique, vintage, and new. She took inspiration from how the light hit each room, choosing brighter colors toward the southern side of the house and a darker, moodier palette on the northern side. Many of the rooms have wallpaper with patterns that echo the surrounding landscape. The house feels generous and welcoming, but also intriguing and sophisticated. It is a testament to the seamless way Heide and Rafe work together, creating seductive environments that transcend the sum of their beautiful parts.

# Main Floor Plan

1. Living Room
2. Front Hall
3. Den
4. Dining Room
5. Powder Room
6. Pantry
7. Kitchen
8. Laundry Room
9. Mudroom
10. Sunroom

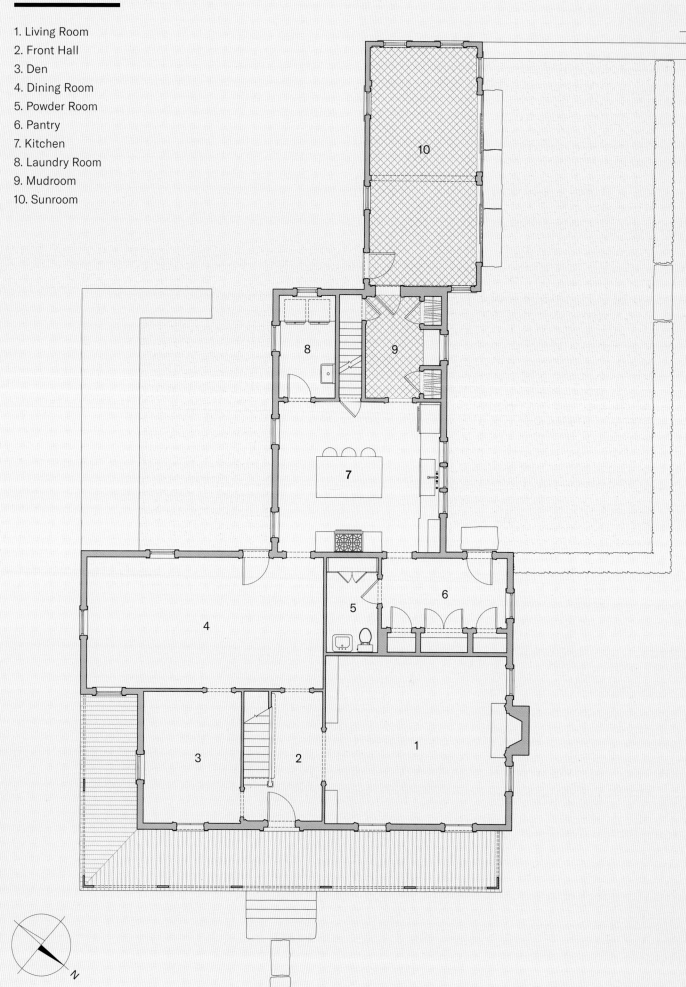

# Upper Floor Plan

1. Primary Bedroom
2. Stair Hall
3. Guest Bedroom
4. Hollis's Bedroom
5. Bathroom
6. Primary Bathroom
7. Rufus's Bedroom
8. Back Hall
9. Guest Bedroom

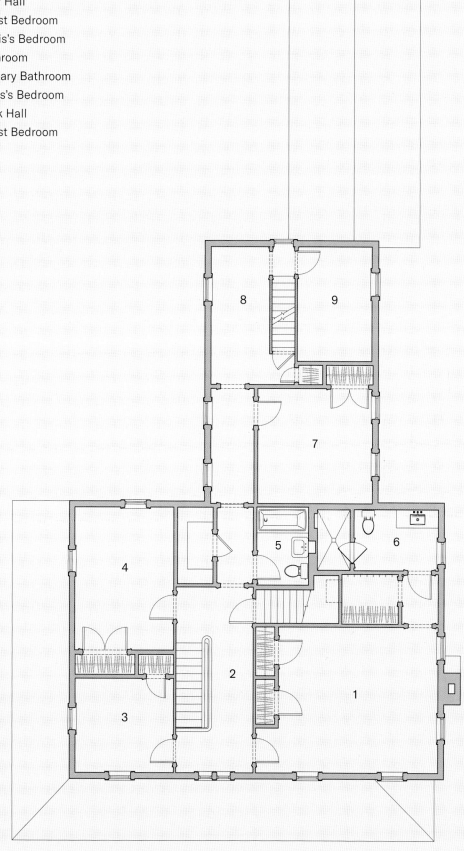

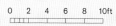

# Gather

To be alone at home is one thing—to hunker down, or to drift idly from room to room. But to be in the company of just one other person changes everything. Inhabiting spaces together, comfortably, requires not only an artful arrangement of furniture but also insight into how people interact. Around a hearth, a table, a kitchen island. In pursuit of coziness, entertainment, collaboration. At Ellsworth, there is no lack of richly appointed configurations that beckon you to sit, lounge, ponder, or engage. Each one is a glorious affirmation of the human impulse to congregate. Though less formal than other homes, there is nevertheless a respectful nod to the shared rituals and traditions—drinking, dining, viewing, listening—that invite us to gather

# *The* Front Hall

### Rafe

Having walked through the house several times before making an offer, I had a pretty good sense of what I wanted to do—although the biggest move in the front hall was suggested by our eleven-year-old son. It was the day of the closing, and we'd finally brought the kids over for a walk-through. Rufus walks in and says, "So we're going to open this up, right? I mean, that's what we do." Adding a large, cased opening from the entry hall to the living room was a key decision. The running trim on the new framework was milled by custom knives cut to match the existing profiles.

The floor of the front hall was covered in a red shag carpet. Not only did Heide and I have an immediate response to the dirty old carpeting, but so did Daisy, our wheaten terrier—she hadn't been in the house more than a minute before marking her new territory. We replaced the sloppily patched flooring below the vintage shag with antique chestnut floorboards from the upper floor of the attached barn at the back of the house. Although the details on the exposed stair stringer came during a previous renovation, we opted to leave them untouched and to accept the quirky additions of applied scrollwork from a previous generation.

### Heide

I have always loved antique rugs. Over the years, I've learned so much about my preferences from one of my favorite rug vendors, Sammy Soheil. He's educated me on the different styles and designs and explained the evolution of the industry. Turns out I have a sweet spot for Kazak, Serapi Heriz, Soumak, and Bakhtiari carpets, especially if made before 1920, when the industry started to commercialize; hand-knotted carpets and natural vegetable dyes then gave way to industrial looms and man-made materials. You'll see mostly antique rugs throughout our home, and when we welcome guests through the front door, this gorgeous Kazak of brick red and teal blue sets the tone. The large terra-cotta olive oil pot was a Christmas present from Rafe. He found it at Michael Trapp's nearby barn, an emporium of treasures.

Throughout our projects, especially when working with older homes, we like to bring in contemporary lighting. It is a surefire way to help a house look of-the-moment, despite its layers of vintage and antique finds against backdrops that seem authentically historic. In the front hall, we hung a pendant from Original BTC; for continuity, we have the same fixture in the upstairs hallway (see page 118). The quality of craftsmanship is excellent, and the subdued ambient light emitted through the handmade porcelain disks can be very soft and romantic in the evening.

# *The* Living Room

Rafe

I mentioned earlier that it was Rufus who came up with the idea of a large cased opening between the front hall and the living room. To further organize the room, we removed three other interior doors, making space for the bookcase and facilitating a more flexible furnishing layout.

Despite the existing door and window trim being more elaborate than what's found in the rest of the house, the room still lacked the desired sense of formality. We had designed a bookcase for another house in Sharon with identical millwork detailing, so we had a head start with that. The bookcase surround at the cased opening is a significant feature, but it is the new window that we installed to the left of the fireplace that really makes the room come to life. Reflected natural light and views across the open fields make this room a favorite in the winter. The final move was to design a crown molding and box beam pairing that not only relates nicely to the existing millwork but also manages the imposing scale of the large, flat ceiling. After living with the wallpaper for a few years, we decided to add it to the ceiling to complete the encompassing, warm, and eclectic vibe of the interior.

Heide

The living room has the only fireplace in the house, and it faces northwest. For these reasons, I knew we would want to spend a lot of time in this space in the winter months and that dark, moodier colors would look even better by firelight. I fully embraced a rich palette of colors and patterns and overfilled the room with intriguing decor. I wanted to be as entertained when nestled in front of the fireplace with a good book as I would be gazing around the room while enjoying a glass of wine and Greg Brown on the speakers.

Much of the furniture in this room came from our previous homes, including the antique easel that Rafe's dad gave him when he graduated from Bennington, but I also enjoyed the hunt for pieces new to us that would be specific to the vibe of this house. I was excited when Ryan Wagner at Pasture Antiques texted me a picture of an early twentieth-century tufted chesterfield sofa. Its perfectly aged velvet upholstery, covered by a sumptuous alpaca throw, is juxtaposed with modern Barcelona chairs and a Paul McCobb stone-top coffee table that sits on an antique Russian Soumak rug. I'm quite proud that this space feels like we inherited the furniture with this house that had been in the same family for multiple generations.

# *The* Den

Rafe

We call this the den, but in reality, it's more like the TV room. Although one of my favorite rooms for its floor-to-ceiling windows, great morning light, and boldly patterned curtains, it serves only one purpose—watching movies.

During the construction phase of the project, we had removed the doorframe separating this room from the dining room. I was happy to see one less doorframe in the dining room and, realizing this space would be mostly used for watching movies, I wanted the den separated from the dining room and the TV out of sight.

Well, that plan changed when Heide showed up and insisted that we rebuild the doorframe and the open connection to the dining room. Butchie Deak, a trusted local carpenter, was quick to side with Heide and actually went on to stress the importance of seeing the kids from the kitchen and dining room. Almost excited for the challenge, he put the doorframe back together—with extra trim we had recently made to match existing elements—and looking like it had always been there.

Heide

I love the diminutive size of this cozy pink room and how it serves a singular function. Our Blu Dot sectional is scaled for a little New York City apartment, so it is perfectly sized to fit in this space and accommodate our family of four, indulging our latest Netflix obsession. I recently added a large ottoman for the latecomer, who missed out on the chaise, to still be able to stretch out and put their feet up. It is made with pink fabric by St. Frank. The simple, handwoven vintage Turkish kilim has an earthy color, which serves as a neutral background to let the wonderful Tree of Life pattern of the Claremont fabric, used for the curtains, be the focus in the room.

We have artwork throughout our home that we've collected over time, and here you see a portrait my mother did of me when I was thirteen years old. I still remember posing for it; when she revealed it to me I was so happy she included my turtle ring!

# *The* Dining Room

Rafe

Initially, there was talk of breaking this room up into two spaces. Ultimately, we kept the large rectangular plan, but simplified its flow. The original dining room had six doorways. After eliminating the three that seemed unnecessary, as well as removing doors from two openings, we finally felt like we could see the potential of the room. We replaced the exterior door leading to the front porch with a new window. The window at the east end offers a view of the grape arbors beyond, planted by the previous owners. Each fall the arbors are weighed down with Concord grapes, a morning snack when heading out to the pool for some of the season's last laps.

With each new window or door, we replicated the existing millwork in its respective room. In this way, we left little trace of our intervention. It was our goal to renovate this house, but to do so without disrespecting the unique inconsistencies found throughout. At times, this meant replicating trim profiles that we may have thought were too big or even clumsy, but it's these unpretentious and honest details that really give the house its character.

Heide

This room is really a dining hall, not a dining room. It has windows and doors on both of its longer sides, and its shorter width is the central axis between the front and back of the house. We knew we needed a long harvest table, so commissioning Chris Harter to make a Shaker-style trestle table was a no-brainer. A brass Lambert & Fils fixture hangs above. The large pigment relief print depicting the cross section of an ash tree is by Bryan Nash Gill. Since the space is central in the floor plan—but also gets some of the best daylight, thanks to windows on three sides—it was destined to get a lot of use. We opted to create a sitting area at the far end to draw people over to share a ray of sun with Mr. Biggie, our cat. The chain-link-base coffee table, sourced from our friends at RT Facts, lends an informal vibe to the sitting area with its antique furniture beautifully reupholstered in handwoven Scalamandré and Claremont fabrics. The wallpaper in this room, Harvest Hare by Mark Hearld, was chosen because it reflects the surrounding landscape. Another remarkable resource for antiques (and owned by a dear old friend) is the George Champion Modern Shop in Woodbury, Connecticut, which is where we found the antique No. 4 Shaker chairs, with their original webbed seats, and the modern Børge Mogensen Shaker dining chairs with original paper cord seats. The Shaker blanket chest was secured by Rafe at an annual auction at Hancock Shaker Village.

# *The* Kitchen

### Rafe

Although we approached the interior renovation conservatively, with a desire to retain the plaster walls and existing trim, we did need to fully gut the kitchen and bathrooms. A kitchen renovation requires all of the trades and eventually becomes the most invasive scope of work for a single room. In the end, we kept the existing heart pine floors; everything else was removed and replaced with new items.

Once the mechanical systems were complete, walls insulated and eventually sheathed, it was a pleasure to watch the room transform from what was considered by most to be a terrifying mess. The custom Statuarietto marble sink really demands attention and prompts our guests to ask why it's so big. Having done a similar sink for a client's farmhouse, it was clear we needed to have our own. Heide's desire to hang our new Falk copper pots on the wall was a move both practical and beautiful. Concerned about the potential clutter, I did push back a bit, but mostly I didn't want to damage the newly plastered walls. Eventually, we settled on beadboard paneling for two of the walls.

### Heide

In the kitchen, my focus was on finishes and lighting. One of my approaches is to establish a recurring palette of colors throughout the house. I especially like to carry at least one or two colors from one room to the next. Here, Farrow & Ball's Dead Salmon on the island is a nod to the Setting Plaster pink in the den just down the hall. The gloss finish helps bounce the light around the room. De Nimes blue, also from Farrow & Ball, on the cabinets and beadboard is also used in the adjacent pantry, demarcating utilitarian functions in the house.

I challenged a convention by picking blue, knowing it is not recommended as a kitchen or dining room color since it is said to be an appetite suppressant. In fact, we came to admit that the space always felt cold and a little too utilitarian. We didn't ever seem to linger longer than getting our work done or our meal made. Even so, I wasn't ready to give up the pretty shade of blue—especially the way it worked with the Original BTC pendants and Heide Martin's stools—so instead, we opted to install Soane's Dianthus Chintz wallpaper on the small areas of white plaster in the room. Its delicate floral block print warms up the entire kitchen, enveloping you in a fresh, summery vibe.

# *The* Pantry

Rafe

The previous owners used this area as a laundry room, but because of its proximity to the back terrace, we wanted the walk through this space to be a bit more special. We needed a pantry that would maximize storage while conveniently concealing the actual use of the space. Originally, we had planned for floor-to-ceiling cupboards, but that didn't work with our budget. Instead, we opted to build out three closets with open shelving behind closed doors. As a simple flourish (that also adds a bit of natural ventilation), we cut out a decorative motif in each door. Following the precedent of the kitchen walls and giving the pantry a more connected feel, we continued the beadboard throughout to define the space as utilitarian. The tombstone glass door that leads to the back terrace was relocated from the dining room. It had been used as an exterior door to the front porch. As in most of the house, the pine floors were repaired and sanded to expose the fresh tone of old-growth eastern white pine.

Heide and I feel that a laundry room should be treated, like a pantry, the same as more visible rooms. The laundry—located just off the kitchen and with a good amount of natural light—is not only durable but also vibrant in both daytime and nighttime. Drawing attention to this utilitarian space may not be a common approach, but we love how the bright color (Farrow & Ball's Sudbury Yellow) pairs with the blue of the kitchen.

Heide

We first painted this room in Farrow & Ball's Borrowed Light, a lighter version of the kitchen's blue tone and intended to bring a fresh, clean feeling to the pantry. Or so I thought. Rafe disliked the shade, which always felt too cool and quiet to him. I didn't want to spend the time and money repainting, but really I still loved the color. So, one morning over coffee, we came up with a compromise. We would bring the darker shade of De Nimes from the kitchen and run it up the Borrowed Light wall to look like a waterline. Problem solved, marriage saved! It also sets the stage for the artwork on the wall, including the Colleen McGuire painting of our last house and a steamship painting by Duncan Hannah.

Off the pantry you can see the little powder room with its Chestnut wallpaper by Marthe Armitage. We love Waterworks and used their porcelain Alden pedestal sink and clean-lined Henry faucet (also seen in the kitchen). Rafe designed the built-in cupboard to make paper goods and cleaning supplies accessible, denying us any excuse for not cleaning up.

# *The* Mudroom

Rafe

Never big enough, a mudroom needs to work for everyone inhabiting and visiting a house. This can seem like an ambitious requirement, but we were determined to get close. With two closets and several feet of hanging space, we were able to include a nearly adequate amount of clothing storage (though more would have been nice). As with the kitchen wall paneling used as a backdrop for our copper pots, durability was a requirement. With beadboard walls and a cement tile floor, this space has stood up nicely to plenty of mud, snow, and Daisy's occasional shake-off.

Even today, it's hard to believe the mudroom has four doors and a cased opening—it's no wonder storage was tough. With the only basement staircase located behind one of the four doors in the room, this has become a high-traffic area for pets, service work, and everyday life.

Heide

Another one of my approaches to selecting paint colors is to make the everyday entry to a house—typically the mudroom in New England—a darker shade. Here we used Mole's Breath, a drab, subterranean shade of gray from Farrow & Ball. Especially if it is a small room, a darker color conceals the inevitable wear and tear on the walls and floor that result from the comings and goings with messy gear, but it also gives your eyes a chance to adjust from the outdoors. The next room you pass into—in this case the kitchen on one side and the sunroom on the other—immediately feels even bigger and brighter.

# *The* Sunroom

Rafe

As a third-generation builder—and having lived through several renovations as a kid—I fully expected some part of the house to be unfinished when we moved in. Eventually, it became obvious: the unfinished part would be the small barn at the back. Although one of my favorite parts of the house, it was just too much work to include in the original scope. Because the space was so small, with ceilings too low even for Heide, we opted to completely gut the interior and expose the timber-frame structure. The chestnut flooring was repurposed in the front hall and laundry room. The interior doors now serve as worktables in the barn, and the hardware was used throughout the house.

When the timber frame was exposed, we wrapped the structure in reinforced plastic to keep it dry and filled it with whatever didn't find a place inside the house or in a storage container. Nearly eighteen months after moving into the main house, we started the renovation of what would become our sunroom. This required rebuilding the fieldstone foundation, pouring a concrete slab, making repairs to the timber frame, sheathing walls, installing windows and doors, adding insulation, and plastering walls. Finished in time for our third winter, the sunroom has become the most beloved room in the house.

Heide

Our previous family home was a wonderfully modest 1920s farmhouse with a little glass-enclosed side porch where we'd huddle with the kids through the long New England winters. When we were finally ready to take on the attached barn space at Ellsworth, I couldn't wait to create another sunroom, this time with a bit more square footage. I also hoped to recapture a moment from my twenties, when I visited a wonderfully eccentric family whose multigenerational home had an orangerie. I was gobsmacked by this exotic space with its citrus trees that had been growing for decades in the dirt floor. I told Rafe it was time for our own orangerie, one so overloaded with potted trees and ungainly house plants we'd have to chop our way to a sunny spot on the sofa to while away our sacred family Sundays.

The vibe of this room skews more modern than the rest of the house. The clean lines of the stone-topped Saarinen table pair beautifully with the California modern lines of the Cleo Baldon dining chairs. Above is an intentionally outsized Baba Tree basket electrified by PET Lamp. Despite its outsized proportion, it twirls delightfully with the slightest breeze. In the sitting area, a 1970s leather de Sede sectional is the perfect backdrop for a 1930s etched-brass table by Philip and Kelvin LaVerne.

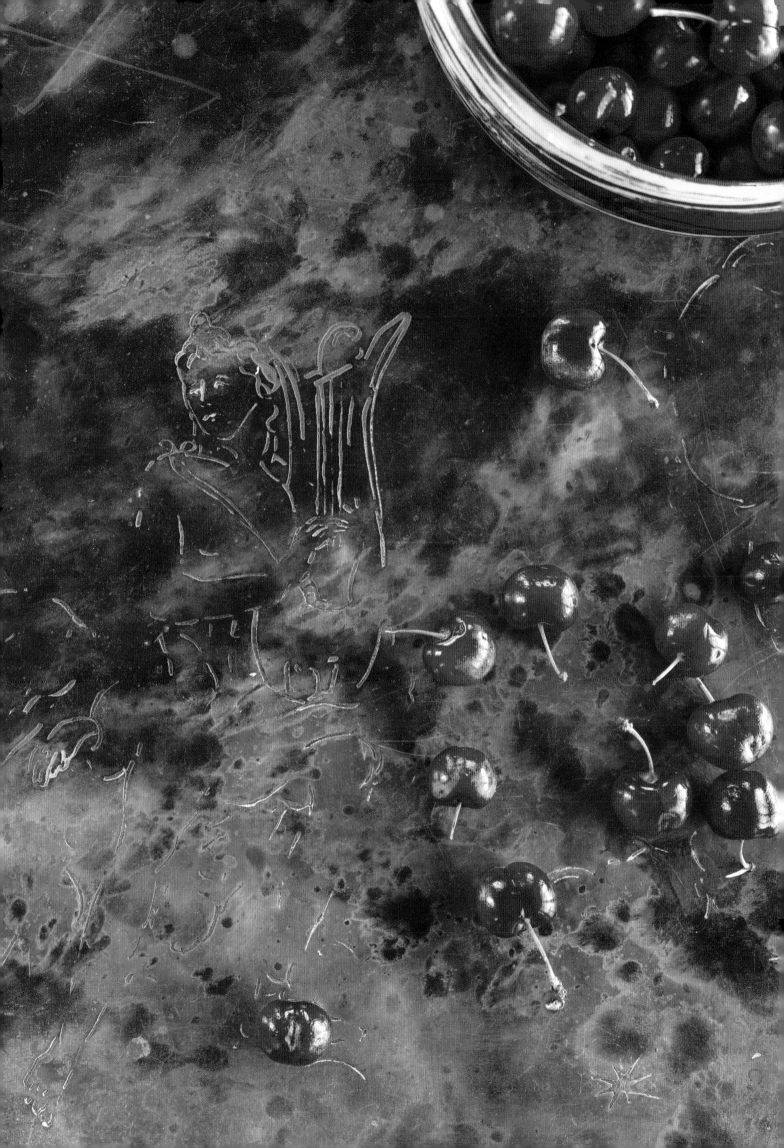

# *The* Terraces

Rafe

Outdoor spaces can get expensive and therefore pushed down the list of priorities. Heide and I decided to keep the outdoor spaces simple and without hardscape, new stone walls, or overly ambitious landscaping. Two terraces, one on each side of the kitchen, provide us with very different experiences and nicely integrate with the flow of the house.

As time went on, we felt the need for additional privacy and added a row of yews along the pea gravel border of the west terrace. Planted as fairly mature shrubs, the evergreens allowed us to quickly realize our goal of a private outdoor space. With time, the hedgerow will fill in and eventually be shaped into a decorative topiary silhouette.

With just pea gravel and reclaimed stone steps, these simple spaces still became a favorite spot to hang out. Heide has continued to arrange these outdoor rooms, bringing in potted plants that create a sense of intimacy. During the fall months, these plants are moved to the sunroom, where they offer a wonderful indoor-outdoor experience during the cooler weather.

Heide

I may not be much of a gardener, but I've learned a good way to cheat is with an effortless pea gravel terrace. For someone like me, who likes to arrange furniture and potted plants, pea gravel is like a blackboard that you can doodle all over and then wipe clean to do it all again. I love an outdoor space furnished with teak, iron, mahogany, and terra-cotta—materials that grow more beautiful with the patina of time and harsh New England weather. My sister, Marie Christine Hendricks, first showed me how expressive plants can be in establishing a mood. She's taken our arrangements to a new level by creating outdoor rooms with walls of plants. I often have to remind myself how grateful I am when I'm out there watering plants for the third hour on Sundays.

# *The* Firepit

### Rafe

One day, Rufus and I decided it was time for a firepit. I'm proud to say that within about twenty minutes, he had collected a dozen medium-sized stones and was ready for my help determining the location. With a two-foot piece of rebar, a length of string, and a screwdriver, we found the center and spun the string and screwdriver from the piece of rebar. A four-foot circle was scratched in the topsoil and the stones laid down. This primitive firepit eventually received a reclaimed steel basin that would accommodate larger fires and, some would say, even looks a little better. However, this is an ongoing discussion.

### Heide

I sincerely hope that the global pandemic brought its own silver-lining moments to everyone. In our case, it was the unexpected family time that we would have with our teenage kids. We moved into this home just before Christmas 2018, and just a few weeks later, Hollis went off to live at school and Rufus disappeared into his bedroom. The lockdown a couple months later brought us all together again in a way that allowed us to christen our home as a concentrated hub of activity during those few months. One of my favorite experiences was snuggling around the firepit in March and April, nestled into sheepskins and blankets, so grateful to be out of the house. Today, the firepit remains our favorite way to entertain family and friends. It brings its own fanfare to an evening and has a casual ease that takes all the stress out of entertaining. Here we have an assembled set of timeworn Adirondack-style chairs along with contemporary mahogany ones made by Rafe's brother Seth. The large rustic console table is one of many finds from Montage Antiques in Millerton, New York.

# Retreat

Whether you ascend the front staircase or sneak up the narrow steps from the kitchen, what awaits on the second floor is a warren of charming rooms dedicated to private pursuits. How we feather our nests says everything about who we are deep down. Art and richly patterned textiles enliven the spaces, alluding to the dreams and proclivities of their inhabitants. Layers of treasures, saturated colors, and disparate elements are woven together to spark familiar memories and evoke distant places and times. Rooms for repose and contemplation, for study and dreaming, must be at once soothing and stimulating. Upstairs at Ellsworth, the eye is delighted at every turn, and a cocoon of sensual pleasures offers the perfect retreat.

# *The* Primary Suite

### Rafe

Our bedroom is one of the larger rooms in the house and by far the most generous bedroom. This might be an obvious choice for the primary suite, but at first, I was considering the back of the house for its privacy and views. Eventually, I agreed with Heide that the additional floor-space was useful to frame a pair of closets sheathed in beadboard paneling. As in the living room, we added a new window to the south side of the chimney, and now we can't imagine the room without its western views of the open farm fields. Through the windows on the north side, the street side, large maple and horse chestnut trees shield us with just enough privacy.

In our previous house, we used our freestanding clawfoot tub only about seven times in eight years, so we decided to forgo a bathtub. With that extra space, Heide got a generous walk-in closet with double hanging rods, a line of Shaker pegs, and a set of integral drawers that extend below the attic staircase. In the bathroom, I had planned for above-sink sconces with bulbs pointing down and installed the junction boxes accordingly. Without knowing this, Heide fell in love with a pair of polished-nickel sconces from Waterworks. After installation, I found them to be too high on the wall and too ostentatious. Rather than tearing open the wall and moving them, I opted for another approach. When Heide was away for a long weekend, I painted the sconces to diminish their presence. While they're still not quite perfect, Heide agrees the look is more interesting.

### Heide

Our bedroom continues to evolve as we live in it. It's where we spend most of our time, so it follows that making it entirely our own should take the longest. The most recent addition is this handmade Italian marbleized paper that we bought from Berdoulat. We had our paperhanger friend, David Devos, install the 16-by-20-inch sheets of paper in a grid pattern so you can see the joints amid the indigo bubbles and swirls. The custom headboard is in Neisha Crosland's Hedgehog fabric, a delightfully whimsical pattern. It's surprisingly versatile and is seen here with Once Milano linens and an antique Souzani rug from John Robshaw's shop in nearby Falls Village.

The vintage Italian desk was another score from Pasture Antiques, and the modern Pierre Jeanneret chair came by way of Holler & Squall. A new obsession in my projects is freestanding room dividers, and Jomain Baumann's tambour screen with its scalloped top is where it all began. It brings a sultry air to the space that makes me feel like a gravel-voiced screen star from a 1930s film. Another design convention that Rafe and I trot out in nearly every project is the old schoolhouse shades. These cheap and ageless spring-loaded roller shades—in that specific tone of green with a particular string loop—are still made in a local factory in Waterbury.

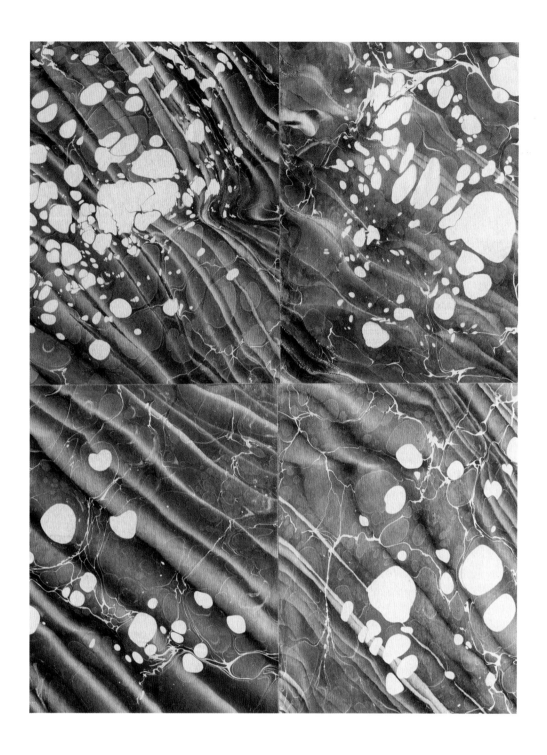

# Hollis's Bedroom

Rafe

It's tough to know how your kids are going to claim their respective bedrooms when moving into a new house. In this case, Hollis, our older child, was quick to claim her room and direct Rufus down the hall. Her room is a classic farmhouse corner bedroom with two windows, closets at an interior wall, and the door conveniently located within the central stair hall. The work done in this room was typical for this project. We built a double-door closet, installed beadboard paneling on the closet wall, added crown molding, sanded the floors, repaired plaster, and gave everything a fresh coat of paint.

The room was originally a bit larger, with an additional fifty square feet she was hoping would serve as an intimate niche for her bed. Instead, we claimed the space for a generous linen closet off the stair hall.

Heide

Hollis's bedroom is distinctly her own. We moved into the house just as she was heading off to school and feared she wouldn't connect with the house, given that her childhood years were spent in another place. The lockdown that arrived a few months later allayed those concerns. She hunkered down and not only made the space her own with her unique decorations and styling but also created a small replica of her room, which she keeps at the foot of her bed. It captures so many little details, right down to the Shantell Martin print on the wall and the vintage Moroccan rug patterns.

# Rufus's Bedroom

### Rafe

After being sent down the hall to find his bedroom, Rufus was quick to realize he had scored the most private room with arguably the best view. He didn't ask for much more than blue trim and the Cole & Son's Woods wallpaper from his previous bedroom. The original space was more of a large open room connecting hallways. Although the open layout of the larger room had a cool flop-house vibe, we opted for adding an interior wall to create his bedroom. The resulting side hallway is a bit longer than we might have liked, but it gives the upstairs a warrenlike feel—a layout any old-house enthusiast can appreciate.

### Heide

Like so many teenagers, Rufus loves his stuff, doesn't clean up much, and always keeps the door closed. Whatever goes on in there—doing homework, FaceTiming friends, playing video games—is entirely his business. Like his sister, Rufus has a cool style of dressing that is a form of self-expression. Similar to other kids of their generation, he has a kind of street style that has nothing to do with the conventional desire to display status. A bit of a pack rat, Rufus holds on to everything. Years ago, we made these large sham covers out of indigo stripe African kuba cloth. They have literally become the fabric of his life, following him to camp, a year at boarding school, and three family homes. They're now a bit threadbare in sections, but nothing a needle and thread can't fix.

# *The* Guest Bedrooms

Rafe

Two guest bedrooms bring us to a total of five bedrooms, plus a finished attic. I'm still hoping for the bedroom across the hall from ours to become a small gym. By *gym* I mean the Peloton, an exercise mat, and some weights. Heide loves the pair of little guest bedrooms.

What better opportunity for an interior designer to create sweet little spaces for our guests? We don't have many overnight visitors, but when our kids have friends over, every sofa and bed is utilized. Many comment on the joy of staying in these delightful little rooms.

Heide

I don't approach guest rooms by trying to appeal to everyone who might stay there. Instead, I see them as an opportunity to showcase dazzling fabrics, wallpapers, and paint colors that we adore but worry might be too much for everyday life—like a graphic Antoinette Poisson wallpaper based on an eighteenth-century French pattern. We also accentuated the tininess of one guest room by filling it with an Early American canopy bed. When you snuggle down under the quilt, you feel tucked away in your own private jewel box.

# *The* Back Hall

**Rafe**

This area is the result of creating a bedroom for Rufus and a little guest bedroom at the top of the back stairs. Keeping the back stairs is a decision we're still thrilled about, although it meant passing on a third full bathroom for the kids or guests. We really have no interest in multiple bathrooms en suite or even additional shared bathrooms. A third full bathroom would have been nice, but keeping up with two and a half is really enough. We figured that if you're staying with us, you must be a good friend and will accept that sharing a bathroom with our kids is just part of the experience.

**Heide**

I like to make hallways feel like little rooms. Why not set one up to invite spontaneous activity? This approach appeals to my fleeting attention span. It's quite pleasant to look down the long corridor and see Hollis or Rufus working at the desk on a watercolor or with LEGO bricks, or Rafe napping in the Sasquatch chair, one of the many amazing antiques from Holler & Squall. (Rafe has an uncanny ability to nap on any surface and in any position!) The sculpture above the chair is by artist James Walsh. He gave it to us on our wedding day; fittingly, it's titled *Foundation* and is made of vestigial building materials he gathered in his Poughkeepsie, New York, neighborhood.

# Wander

The moment you step outside the main house at Ellsworth, another world presents itself. Right away, the porch, with its charming original scrollwork, offers a civilized perch from which to consider the day or read a book. Ways of interacting with the land change with the seasons. Follow the stone path out front to picnic under the spreading branches of the horse chestnut. Pick apples, snowshoe across the field, convene for hot toddies around the fire, gaze up at the stars, swim laps in the pool. Stroll out to the barn for work or play, or continue into the woods and wetlands beyond, where bitter-sweet and grape vines twine over sugar maple, black cherry, and ash trees. The house is a beacon, but the surrounding landscape is always a reason to wander.

# *The* Outdoors

Rafe

Although Heide and I first saw the farmhouse nearly twenty years ago, it wasn't until we were within a year of buying it that I really began to understand the property. Although a farmhouse with additions is common among New England agricultural properties, Ellsworth has a similar composition to those found in New Hampshire, Maine, and even as far afield as Nova Scotia. The historical precedent of "big house, little house, back house, barn" is one that I have always loved. The house not only sits among significant maple trees but also tells a story of multiple generations living and working on this onetime dairy farm.

We learned that the "big house" originally had shutters, so we decided to restore the ornamentation of the front porch and windows, plus return traditional shutters to the windows. While we replaced all the windows on the "little house," we did keep the existing trim details and pared-down exterior without shutters or ornamentation. What is now the sunroom can easily be seen as the "back house," clearly the simplest building on the property.

I love a landscape of mature plantings but have no interest in the maintenance required to keep things thriving. Instead, I look to tall grass, selective mowing, stone walls, and fruit trees to create a naturalistic landscape. With eighteen acres of open farmland and fifteen acres of dense woodlands, there are endless possibilities for working with the natural landscape. The first thing we did when we bought the house was to clear decades of overgrowth from several thousand feet of historic stone walls.

A local farmer continues to hay the fields of timothy grass for use as fodder at a nearby dairy farm. After a year of living on the property, I decided it was time to take over the maintenance of the site out of a desire to connect with it more deeply. Each spring, I select new paths to be mowed through the farm fields, maintain the clearing of the stone walls, and continue to blaze trails through the woodlands.

There are only two outbuildings on the property; both had small additions in total disrepair that we eventually removed. The result is two freestanding barns, rectangular in footprint and monolithic in form. Running with the "down east" vibe of the property, we used white cedar shingles on the side walls of the two barns. As the siding ages, the barns seem to grow roots of their own and continue the story of the old farm.

# *The* Barn

Rafe

There were several parties interested in the property, and each had a special plan to make it their own. The most common strategy was to demolish the dairy barn and move the house farther from the road—the last things we would ever consider. Nevertheless, while we focused on the main house, we were also concerned about the barn collapsing. To prevent this, we had bracing installed and two large brown tarps strapped down over the roof.

Eventually, we were able to pull together the funds for the barn renovation. This included reinforcing the floor system and rafters, and reframing the gable walls. Once the structure was stable, we replaced the roof, exterior trim, windows, and doors, and installed new siding. Our friend Gardner Murray built the large steel-framed windows at each end. This addition transformed the upstairs into the dramatic space we had envisioned.

The barn loft, where the hay was once stored, has high ceilings with a wonderfully ribbed, cavernous feeling. The downstairs of the 32-by-60-foot barn is divided into three long bays: workshop, garage, and general storage for landscaping equipment. Thanks to a pro-pane heater, the workshop and garage have become my go-to places on most weekends and offer a welcome opportunity to work from home.

Heide

Once the barn renovation was under control, it was time to consider how we'd use the space. Back in the mid-1980s, Rafe and his brother Seth had built an 8-foot-tall halfpipe in the woods at their Woodbury, Connecticut, home. Before we moved into Ellsworth, Hollis had already begun to dabble in skating around the neighborhood with fearless downhill runs and longboarding. Wanting a greater challenge, it was time for a ramp of her own. The timing proved auspicious with Covid lockdown. We decided to enhance the clubhouse vibe by installing a projector for which Rafe built a movie-house screen. I found a long emerald-green channel-back banquette at a local auction for $75 and placed a few marble-topped bistro tables for our dinner theater. Off to the sides are comfy down-filled sofas and two pairs of military-style twin beds with footlockers. The space has only become more layered over time as we add in cool finds such as the large tag-sale painting of a seascape, the unusual steel fish-scale chandelier from Holler & Squall, and the purple velvet English armchair. The kids have hosted many parties out there, but I also have an especially fond memory of a raucously fun sleepover with my "Hell Bags" book group!

# Ellsworth Classics

## Rafe

In 2020, I decided to buy a vintage Range Rover. Not a shiny, fully loaded Range Rover, but a 1989 Range Rover Classic in a faded Portofino red. Although great-looking and a pleasure to drive, it is refreshingly simple, somewhat slow, and notoriously lacking in power. In my defense, I feel it's important to mention my disdain for touchscreens, advanced driver-assistance systems, and backup cameras. This wasn't my first Land Rover; I had previously owned a 1997 Range Rover and a 2007 LR3. Both were great cars and never a problem. To be clear, I love these cars, but insist that I am not a "car guy."

I know what it sounds like when I say that I buy and sell these for fun. Of course, I drive them all and love nearly every minute of it. However, when flipping cars, much like houses, there are always surprises. Not every sale is profitable, but in the end my goal is to make a little money, have a bit of fun, and meet some great people with a shared passion.

## Heide

The summer after high school, my friends and I rented a house on Martha's Vineyard where I experienced many new things, including my first big crush, on our neighbor, who drove a vintage Land Rover. The sight of our Series III makes me feel like I'm a teenager again, so I'm happy to have these cars around. For the record, Rafe is so much sexier, smarter, more industrious, and a much better father than my long-ago crush could ever be. (He made me write that last line, but I was about to anyway.)

SYMBOL    IDENTIFICATION

⚠     : WARNING

📖     : REFER TO
        OWNERS
        MANUAL

⚠ 📖 ⊙
POWER STEERING FLUID

# *The* Swimming Pool

Rafe

Never did I think we would have a swimming pool. My father's parents had an above-ground pool when I was a kid, and I loved spending time at their house. Heide and I had barely even considered a pool when the kids were young, given that our serial renovation projects and saving for the kids' education made the expensive maintenance costs prohibitive. After a few successful house sales and several good years at work, we finally indulged in a pool. This was at the height of the pandemic, so our timing wasn't great, but we were thrilled to be swimming by Memorial Day and even hosting small, socially distanced get-togethers. For me, the pool is mostly about the solitary and meditative experience of swimming laps, followed by naps in the cabana. For Heide, it's all about entertaining!

A summer of direct sunlight and more than a little sunburn indicated it was time for a shade structure. I built it of rough-sawn white cedar, with exposed framing clad in 1-by-4 strapping not only to provide shade throughout the day but also to serve as an armature for the climbing wisteria. We imagine the cabana someday covered in the flowering vine and fully shading the interior.

Heide

The pool pavilion is loosely based on the corncribs that you used to see in New England farm pastures, with slatted walls to continuously ventilate the harvested cache of corn. When it came to furnishings, I wanted to keep it simple with things that could live out there all season. An assembled collection of vintage Woodard furnishings was the solution. The pair of 1950s lounge chairs from Regan & Smith in Hudson has cushions made from Dedar's outdoor fabric. I love the cool blue geometric pattern with the bold 1960s orange-and-red geometric pattern on the daybed, a local find from the Millerton Antiques Center. It's a vibrant, noisy mix—like what you'd find at a pool party with guests' inhibitions lowered by Aperol spritzes. The dinette set for light poolside lunches, like all of the other Woodard pieces, was painted a dark blue to unify the collection of varying styles.

# Ellsworth *Flora*

Native and introduced species of plants and trees, including many with edible and medicinal properties, mingle in the sprawling meadows and mixed deciduous forest. They are part of a thriving ecosystem at Ellsworth that also includes insects, birds, and small mammals.

### RED CLOVER
*Trifolium pratense*

This flowering plant has been used to treat respiratory infections, skin inflammation, and symptoms of menopause.

### WHITE CLOVER
*Trifolium repens*

An infusion of this common plant can boost the immune system and help treat fever, cough, colds, and joint pain.

### BROADLEAF PLANTAIN
*Plantago major*

Simply chew a leaf of this fibrous plant to release its juices, then rub on nettle stings, mosquito bites, and even splinters to amazing effect.

### PHILADELPHIA FLEABANE
*Erigeron philadelphicus*

Reputed to have antioxidant and neuroprotective properties, fleabane has been used by Native tribes as an astringent, a diuretic, and an expectorant.

### BITTER DOCK
*Rumex obtusifolius*

This bitter plant is edible as a leafy green or potherb in the early spring, when the leaves are young and tender. It can also be applied topically to treat burns and blisters.

### FRAGRANT BEDSTRAW
*Galium triflorum*

This trailing perennial has a lovely, sweet smell, and the young shoots have a mild, pleasant taste reminiscent of green beans.

### OXEYE DAISY
*Leucanthemum vulgare*

An introduced European species, this cheerful wildflower thrives in sunny meadows. When young and tender, its leaves add sweet flavor to salads.

### WHITE ASH
*Fraxinus americana*

This native tree is a critical food source for frogs and other creatures. Its wood has been used extensively to make sporting goods, including baseball bats.

### SUGAR MAPLE
*Acer saccharum*

Known for its beautiful fall foliage and as the primary source of maple syrup, this native tree can also be tapped in the spring for its refreshing clear sap.

### SUMMER GRAPE
*Vitis aestivalis*

A vigorous vine that produces aromatic fruit, this plant also has edible leaves that can be wrapped around fillings and steamed or baked.

### JEWELWEED
*Impatiens capensis*

The juice squeezed from this plant's tender green leaves and translucent stems helps soothe skin irritations, including rash from poison ivy.

### CANADA GOLDENROD
*Solidago canadensis*

Contrary to popular belief, this plant, which blooms in the fall, does not cause allergies. Its yellow flowering tops can even be made into a tea that reduces seasonal allergies.

### JACK-IN-THE-PULPIT
*Arisaema triphyllum*

This perennial wildflower blooms in spring with a bright green- or purple-striped hood that folds over, evoking a preacher at the pulpit.

### SENSITIVE FERN
*Onoclea sensibilis*

The name of this fern comes from its sensitivity to frost. Its fertile fronds appear in the summer and remain upright through winter with beautiful bead-like spore cases.

### RAMBLER ROSE
*Rosa multiflora*

This Asian species has lovely pale blooms with a light clove scent. In fall and winter, tiny red rose hips, rich in vitamin C, can be harvested to steep for tea.

# A Conversation *between* Heide Hendricks *and* Rafe Churchill

**Rafe**

Do you remember way back, when we were driving up Route 4 from Cornwall with little idea of what was ahead? We were up for the weekend and as usual we were exploring the northwest corner. Instead of continuing up Route 7 along the Housatonic River, we decided to head west and see what was up the hill. When we got to the top of the hill, we found a pair of neighboring farms, a cluster of large barns, and a pond. It was one of those moments when there was more to take in than just our location. In this case, there were no cars around, the late afternoon light was perfect, and the pond on the north side of the road was beautifully surrounded by phragmites. With tall reed grasses on one side and a dilapidated little house sitting close by—it was perfect.

**Heide**

We couldn't believe what we had found, but had to ask, "How could we live here? What would we do for a living?" I loved living in New York and wasn't ready to leave. Sharon, Connecticut, seemed so far from Brooklyn, and making a living was hard enough for us even there.

**Rafe**

Fortunately, we realized it was all about shifting our priorities. Instead of focusing on our careers, we focused on how to make this move happen. OK, to be honest, it was my goal. I had spent so much time trying to convince you of moving to Vermont, but with this new mission I was somehow able to find cheap land only a half a mile away from our inspired spot on the hill.

**Heide**

No doubt Rafe, you knew that we had found something special. Not many people would have found raw land and built a house in time for our first child. From then on it was all about making it work. We prioritized our goal of having a family and a house of our own, while our careers evolved more organically. Fortunately, we both had jobs that allowed us to work remotely and with some flexibility. Today this would be so much easier, but for us it was the challenge that made it even more exciting.

**Rafe**

I think what would surprise people most is to hear that you and I grew up in the same town.

**Heide**

I love saying you're the boy next door I never knew.

**Rafe**

It's not that strange our paths didn't cross, given how different our families were. You had a much more bohemian lifestyle, definitely more art based.

**Heide**

My father was an artist first and foremost, but he undertook the building of our house—even though he'd never built anything in his life—mostly because it was really cheap land. He and my mother showed me and my four siblings that there were no

obstacles or limits if you just approach things as if solving a creative puzzle. And we all had equal investment in this house; we were encouraged to change it in any way that would please us aesthetically. My sister decided she wanted to make a koi pond in the floor of the living room. My brother built a rock wall going up the side of the fireplace with water trickling down. I remember drawing on the walls.

**Rafe**

That sounds like a lot of freedom. How'd that work out?

**Heide**

There was a lot of freedom, but that lifestyle also brought financial hardship. We sometimes struggled to keep the lights on or food in the fridge. So maybe that's partly why I wanted a more reliable income and chose a different path, working as a publicist, having a steady nine-to-five gig. At the same time, it left me unable to walk into a room or a space without looking at it as a potential collage in the making. I can't not be creative. Which probably made it inevitable that I would end up as a designer.

**Rafe**

I really craved that kind of freedom growing up in a somewhat structured, disciplined environment. The houses we lived in were always under construction. We never lived in one that was finished. By the time I was twelve, I was hauling cinder blocks around my father's jobsites. Sometimes I felt I was raised to work in construction, but it never felt like a good fit. Growing up, I had a sense that a life in the trades wouldn't satisfy me, even though it was really all I knew.

**Heide**

By the time we met, you had already graduated from Bennington and wanted to be a sculptor. You were obsessed, always thinking about your next piece, and I found that very attractive. Especially because I didn't have the confidence to make art, although I loved art.

**Rafe**

I had no idea how to turn making art into a career, even though I had some early success with my sculpture. Ultimately, I also lacked self-confidence. I was just too young. Ironically, building was a safe place to retreat. So, I worked as a construction laborer and house painter in high school and college, into my early twenties. There were a few attempts to break away from construction with jobs as a substitute teacher, a metalworker, and a museum educator. I even taught a needle-arts class at the Westover School in Middlebury, Connecticut. But after a couple of years of working at nonprofits—at the Aldrich Contemporary Art Museum and at Westover—I was broke and in debt. Construction was how I could dig myself out of this hole.

**Heide**

It seems incredible that we both ended up where we did, but also kind of inevitable. I don't think I could have become an interior designer any sooner, because it was the journey that paved the way. The whole time I was employed at art galleries and museums or in development departments or as a publicist, I was poring through shelter magazines and cultivating my eye and accumulating experience creating our personal spaces that would ultimately make my pivot to designer very easy. I always had an intuitive skill for spatial organization, and I knew from being an event planner how to organize my approach and how to create floor plans from working with you on our own homes.

**Rafe**

Since we didn't come from money and didn't have any support, we had to really work. Taking on these more mainstream jobs—even though they were in nonprofit or construction—was sort of an attempt to acclimate, to care for ourselves in the only way we'd been taught. We oscillated between that and these side gigs, playing around with where our true passions lay. But it wasn't until I fully left construction behind and you stepped into your role as interior designer that we began to get close to where we are today.

**Heide**

We're very fortunate that we found a way of life that's informed by our lifestyle. We don't really think of work as work—it's what we were always doing, even when we had other jobs. Our passion for what we do, what we're truly good at, is a big part of the reason why we're successful. For me, I think it all started with that first little cottage that we bought and renovated and just made uniquely our own. Even though we were living paycheck to unsteady paycheck, you said we had to do it. Even though it was $30,000.

**Rafe**

They were asking $60,000, and we got it for $30,000. I was really impressed in the early days with the way you had your own tool belt and tools and did demolition and hung drywall and even carried bundles of asphalt shingles up the ladder. Yeah, you were beautiful and had a great sense of humor, but it was your comfort with power tools that really sealed the deal.

**Heide**

Well, I've always appreciated the way you provide the armature, the structure—not only architecturally speaking, but even in our journey in life. You're the one who looks ahead. I remember on one of our first dates, you asked me about my five-year plan. And I couldn't believe it because I was just living in the moment. But soon enough we got into a rhythm of cashing our paychecks every Friday, running to the lumberyard for supplies, and working on whatever cottage renovation we had going all weekend, before heading back to our day jobs on Monday and doing it all over again. It awakened my interest in wanting this life that had begun to seem attainable through our own hard work. I just loved that we could control our destiny.

**Rafe**

Or at least where we slept. Of course, it was simple, but not as easy as it looked.

**Heide**

One house after another, the property would go up in value and the return would be good, which was so empowering. It was incredibly thrilling when the first house we built in Sharon went on the market and sold the very same day—and this was back when real estate was not selling! That's when you and I looked at each other and said, "Okay, I think there's some magic here. I think we might have something special."

**Rafe**

For me, one of the best parts is that I get to work in a creative industry, not only making a good living but also having a good amount of freedom. Ellsworth really feels like an expression of that. Even though we've been here for only a few years, it feels like something new. Like I have a sense of permission to do a little bit more of whatever I want. I enjoy working on the house and finding new projects each spring, but there's also no hurry.

**Heide**

So, I think you're going to like this. For me, Ellsworth represents the first time I could imagine a long-range plan. Only with Ellsworth did I think about the future. I felt that with you creating a solid backdrop and me layering in the color and comfort and patina, our personal home would be the synthesis of our journey together. Every design decision was made so effortlessly, and it's not just because of all these collaborative projects we've done—it's also our shared life experience, where we were with our family and where we were headed.

**Rafe**

Every time I pull off Route 4 heading toward Ellsworth, I still feel that sense of relief, the stress leaves my body. As I look out the window at the tall grass in the sunlight, I know it's going to be hard to find a reason to leave. Our home is a great place for our family to find respite in a private and supportive environment. Come home, recharge, reflect, and then get back to work, because you've got to have a place to go.

# Acknowledgments

In a book that documents our family home, we want to start by thanking our children, Hollis and Rufus, for their invaluable contributions at every stage. For tolerating the seemingly endless conversations about architecture, construction, and interior design. And for the relentless—but fruitful!—search for what has become our shared dream home.

Reaching further back in time, we are so grateful to George and Marie Hendricks, who shaped Heide's vision and launched her into the world from a platform of artists who live to create and create to live surrounded by beauty. Our thanks go to Seth Churchill, for being a true partner and confidant through the most challenging years, and for realizing and accepting that it was time for Rafe to break out and follow his heart. And to Jim and Diane Churchill, for encouraging and fostering Rafe's interest in art and design from an early age. We also thank Theo Coulombe, for his years of friendship and emotional support. And of course, there would be no Ellsworth without our trusted friend Chris Garrity at Bain Real Estate.

There's no denying that ours is a service business and that it's our clients who bestow upon us the opportunity and creative freedom we need to do our best work. It was Matt and Jessie Sheehan who believed in us from the start—in fact, they were our first client and the impetus for us to form a professional team, to launch our firm, to really come into our own. Over the years, so many clients have been kindred spirits, and our journeys together paved the way for Hendricks Churchill to become a firm whose influence extends beyond this little corner of northwest Connecticut.

We wish to thank a very special, well-rounded, and exemplary group that we relied upon at Hendricks Churchill as we endeavored to produce our first book: Patrick Corrigan, James Harris, Ann Hedbavny, Devin Meaney, Lizzie Duffy Morley, William Munn, Sarah Roberts Hale, and Adrienne Sieverding. We also extend our thanks to Pete Hanby, Sarah Haberern, George Rein, and John "Butchie" Deak for their special contributions to the Ellsworth project. For getting the word out about our achievements, there is no one better than the team of DADA Goldberg, a strategic communications agency that saw our potential and helped us soar. We couldn't have done it without founding partner Defne Aydintasbas, a beacon who guided us, and Ethan Elkins, who hunkered down with us in the trenches. We also felt seen and honored by the support of lauded editorial tastemakers at *Architectural Digest, Connecticut Cottages & Gardens, Elle Decor, House & Garden, House Beautiful, Luxe Interiors + Design, Martha Stewart Living, New England Home, The New York Times, Period Homes, The Sunday Times, Vogue,* and *The Wall Street Journal.*

We'd be remiss if we didn't tip our hats to the many sources of inspiration that lit fires within us going back decades. So many visits to historic house museums throughout the United States and Europe, abandoned buildings, and auction houses. And, equally important, the artwork of Helen Frankenthaler, Alexander Calder, Robert Gober, Ann Hamilton, Winslow Homer, H. C. Westermann, Edward Hopper, Peter Poskas, and Andrew Wyeth. In regular rotation on our pinup boards is the work of contemporary architects and designers we admire, including Ilse Crawford, Steven Gambrel, Ben Pentreath, Max Rollitt, Gil Schafer, Dimore Studio, and Faye Toogood.

If ever our confidence wavered, we were heartened by the support of the Institute of Classical Architecture and Art (ICAA), whose esteemed awards offered our nascent design firm important early recognition.

The making of a book is no small undertaking, and we feel honored to have made our first deal at Rizzoli, the most esteemed house for art and architecture publications. We're so lucky that publisher Charles Miers allowed us the freedom to interpret the form and devise our own version of an inspiring design book. With the guidance of Philip Reeser, our insightful and encouraging editor, we have been able to enjoy this new creative process. After featuring us in his inaugural issue as editor in chief of *Elle Decor*, and offering his continued support, Asad Syrkett agreed to distinguish us further by writing the foreword for our debut book. The dream team we put together to bring it to life has made every aspect more compelling. Chris Mottalini has an artist's eye and a rare talent for capturing interiors that feel real and yet elevated by his extraordinary lighting. Laura Chávez Silverman truly has a way with words, always finding a way to articulate what visual people struggle to express. Conor Brady created a spare yet lush design that spotlights our work in a way that makes us proud. And with that, we recall the Shaker maxim, "That is best which works best."

—Heide and Rafe

# Resources

## ANTIQUES AND FURNISHINGS

ANK Ceramics
*ankceramics.com*

Chris Harter
*chrisharter.com*

Cottage+Camp
*cottagecamp.net*

FINCH hudson
*finchhudson.com*

George Champion
Modern Shop
*championmodern.com*

Get Back Inc.
*getbackinc.com*

Hancock Shaker Village
*hancockshakervillage.org*

Heide Martin Design Studio
*heidemartin.com*

Holler & Squall
*hollerandsquall.com*

Hunter Bee
*hunterbee.com*

Michael Trapp
*michaeltrapp.com*

Modern Archive Shop
*modernarchiveshop.com*

Montage Antiques
*montageantiques.com*

Newlyn Lowly Antiques
*instagram.com/newlynlowly*

Regan & Smith
*reganandsmith.com*

RT Facts
*rtfacts.com*

Seth Churchill Furniture
*sethchurchillfurniture.com*

## APPLIANCES

Clarke
*clarkeliving.com*

Falk Culinair
*falkcoppercookware.com*

Miele
*mieleusa.com*

Sub-Zero
*subzero-wolf.com*

Wolf
*subzero-wolf.com*

## DOORS AND WINDOWS

Marvin
*marvin.com*

Murray Workshop
*murrayworkshop.com*

Shuttercraft
*shuttercraft.com*

Simpson Door Company
*simpsondoor.com*

Windsor Windows & Doors
*windsorwindows.com*

## HARDWARE

Horton Brasses
*horton-brasses.com*

House of Antique Hardware
*houseofantiquehardware.com*

Rejuvenation
*rejuvenation.com*

Urban Archaeology
*urbanarchaeology.com*

## LIGHTING

Authentic Designs
*authenticdesigns.com*

David Weeks Studio
*davidweeksstudio.com*

Hector Finch
*hectorfinch.com*

Lambert & Fils
*lambertetfils.com*

Manufactum
*manufactum.com*

Marianna Kennedy
*mariannakennedy.com*

Noguchi Museum
*noguchi.org*

Original BTC
*originalbtc.com*

PET Lamp
*petlamp.org*

Schoolhouse
*schoolhouse.com*

Waterworks
*waterworks.com*

## PAINT AND WALLPAPER

Antoinette Poisson
*antoinettepoisson.com*

Berdoulat
*berdoulat.co.uk*

Cole & Son
*cole-and-son.com*

Farrow & Ball
*farrow-ball.com*

FAYCE Textiles
*faycetextiles.com*

Mark Hearld
*stjudesfabrics.co.uk/
collections/mark-hearld*

Marthe Armitage
*marthearmitage.co.uk*

Soane Britain
*soane.co.uk*

## PLUMBING FIXTURES, FITTINGS, AND BATH ACCESSORIES

Duravit
*duravit.us*

Kohler
*kohler.com*

Waterworks
*waterworks.com*

## SPECIALTY MILLWORK AND CABINETRY

Franklin Hardwood Floors
*franklinwood.com*

Gordon Woodworking
860-489-5445

Hyde Park Mouldings
*hyde-park.com*

Ponders Hollow
*pondershollow.com*

Vermont Farm Table
*vermontfarmtable.com*

## STONE AND TILE

Ann Sacks
*annsacks.com*

Granada Tile
*granadatile.com*

Heritage Tile
*heritagetile.com*

Rock Solid Marble
and Granite
*rocksolidmandg.com*

Stone Curators
*stonecurators.com*

## TEXTILES AND RUGS

Claremont
*claremontfurnishing.com*

Dedar
*dedar.com*

F. Schumacher & Co.
*fschumacher.com*

John Robshaw
*johnrobshaw.com*

Kirsten Hecktermann
*kirstenhecktermann.com*

Neisha Crosland
*neishacrosland.com*

Once Milano
*oncemilano.com*

Perennials
*perennialsfabrics.com*

Scalamandré
*scalamandre.com*

Soheil Oriental Rugs,
Soheil Sasanian
*sorugs@yahoo.com*

## WORKS OF ART

Bryan Nash Gill
*bryannashgill.com*

Colleen McGuire
*cmcguireart.com*

James Walsh
*jameswalshartist.com*

Shantell Martin
*shantellmartin.art*